JOY

Gardens of the Heart

JOY

ELIZABETH CLARE PROPHET

SUMMIT UNIVERSITY PRESS®

GARDINER, MONTANA

JOY
by Elizabeth Clare Prophet
Copyright©2012 Summit Publications, Inc.
All rights reserved

For information, contact Summit University Press,
63 Summit Way, Gardiner, MT 59030.
Tel: 1-800-245-5445 or 406-848-9500
www.SummitUniversityPress.com

Library of Congress Control Number 2012931499
ISBN: 978-1-60988-097-2
ISBN: 978-1-60988-105-4 (eBook)

SUMMIT UNIVERSITY 🐦 PRESS®

Cover and interior design by James Bennett Design

Printed in the United States of America
16 15 14 13 12   5 4 3 2 1

CONTENTS

Approaching the Garden

Everyone yearns for deep and lasting joy. If you look around, though, you see that while some people emanate joy, others wear sullen faces and still others make merry and laugh but seem to lack real joy.

The key to joy is simple. There is only one source of real joy, and it is within you. True joy comes from knowing your inner reality. As you become more and more of who you really are, you no longer depend on outer circumstances for happiness and contentment. You come to know a deep joy that cannot be shaken.

True joy differs from happiness. While happiness often depends on outer circumstances, joy is an inner quietude, an inner sense of well-being.

Your thoughts and feelings affect every cell of your body. When you are filled with joy, the effect on your cells can produce a powerful change that, in some cases, can turn diseased cells back to a state of health.

To maintain inner joy in the face of trials, avoid identifying with the sense of struggle. When you have inner joy, you more easily accept things as they are. You view challenges as opportunities to grow, to learn, and to look within for creative solutions. Instead of reacting to what others say or do, you focus on the good and let the rest go. This takes self-control and it builds self-mastery. Over time, you learn to trust that focusing on the good allows that goodness to carry you through to resolution and greater joy.

To experience the miracle of joy, let yourself become excited about the good things and the beautiful things you see. When you have inner joy, that joy naturally spreads to everyone around you. As you share joy with others, your joy will increase even more.

THE TRELLIS

Joy is an inner quietude

that anchors and centers you

in the great web of life.

Joy blossoms when you accept

the things you cannot change

and work to change for the better

the things you can.

Within your heart is the source

of joy, equanimity, and bliss.

You can tap it at any time,

regardless of outer circumstances.

Let a fountain of joy

flow within and through you,

displacing a dependence on others

for happiness and contentment.

Joy in the heart

kindles the fire of creativity

and opens the door

to finding creative solutions

to life's challenges.

Joy is the motor of life

and the foundation of healing.

It takes joy to fully release

your cares and burdens.

It takes joy to desire to live,

to will to live.

Joy comes from being connected

to your inner reality.

No matter what task or activity

you are engaged in,

you can live in a state of joy.

Let your joy be perpetual!

You are joy.

You are beauty.

You are wholeness.

Nothing that is within you

can be taken from you.

Cultivate joy in every area

of your life.

Count your joys as you would

count your blessings.

The potential for joy

is everywhere.

Joy comes from living

in harmony with nature.

Any task can be a joyful

expression of who you are.

You can affirm your real self

in whatever you do.

The joy in doing anything

is in doing it

to the best of your ability.

If you have ever watched

a two-year-old clap for joy

upon doing something

new and wonderful,

you have seen the joy

that comes from

a sense of achievement.

Discover the joy that can be yours

when you strive and give your best.

Joy is movement and life.

Joy is giving attention

to the needs of your body.

Joy is a key to your healing.

You must bring joy to your life,

joy to your plants and joy to your goldfish.

You must be a dispenser of joy.

And when people see you coming, they'll say,

"Why, the sun just came out.

The sun came into my room."

And that will be the truth because

joy is the sun of your heart.

Joy is the divine champagne

that bubbles over hearts

till the soul laughs within itself

at all outer conditions.

Joy is the bubbling

within your consciousness

that dispels darkness,

doubt, and fear,

and guides you toward

your inner reality.

Joy can be seen in a smile

and heard in a voice—

and that joy is contagious.

Become an invincible

manifestation of joy

that nothing can move

or turn aside.

Light a candle of joy

for life.

SONGBIRDS

Joy is without price,

for it comes directly

from the heart.

To increase your joy,

visualize a waterfall

of iridescent light

bathing and regenerating

your being and world,

flowing through you at all times.

Accept the joy it brings.

Recall the joy you feel

in seeing the stars at night,

smelling a rose,

walking in nature.

Your joy is a reflection

of what is within you.

Some people make merry

without having any real joy.

Inner joy comes from knowing

that you are fulfilling

your reason for being.

Align with the joy

that can be yours.

See each challenge as leading you,

one step at a time,

to a higher level of your being.

Use challenges as opportunities

to cultivate joy.

Meet each challenge with joy.

Joy is an energy of excitement,

of expecting good things

to enter your life.

Joyous expectancy

keeps your goals alive

and keeps you engaged.

Joy brings energy for living.

If joy is missing from your life,

ask yourself whether there is

someone you need to forgive

or ask to forgive you.

Being at peace with yourself

and with others

keeps the joy fountain flowing.

Fear, doubt, and anxiety

disturb your being and block

abundance and joy.

Restore inner peace

by stilling the troubled waters

of your being

and you will be able to see

the reflection of the good

and the joy that await you.

If you experience loss,

let yourself feel the sorrow

before gently moving on.

Whenever joy flees from your

heart and mind, go within.

Reconnect to your inner reality.

In the darkest night, joy can come

as a sign of profound resolution,

balance, and peace.

Learn to share nuggets of truth

with sensitivity and hope.

Share in a way that offers

a burst of awareness.

Speak words that bring joy

and comfort to others.

Little things bring great joy—

a kind gesture, a smile,

a handful of flowers from

a radiant-faced child.

It is the sweet, simple things

that bring deep and lasting joy.

Joy is like helium in a

giant balloon carrying you aloft—

if your joy starts to go down,

you have to throw out

some of the ballast.

Allow the sun to wipe away

doubt, fear, and worry.

Take a sun bath.

Feel the sun's healing rays

bathing and renewing

your body, mind, and being.

Allow the sun to restore in you

feelings of childlike joy.

When you feel a spontaneous

burst of joy from seeing

the twinkle in someone's eye

or hearing a delightful remark,

claim it.

Go deeply into the feeling

until you are literally

vibrating with joy.

Prime the pump

until the water of joy flows.

People seek various answers

to life's challenges,

but what we all want

is to find and keep joy.

Maintaining inner joy

takes work on ourselves,

our interactions with others,

our responses to whatever

someone might say or do.

Keep your thoughts light.

Let go of gossip, criticism,

and judgment.

Seeing and supporting

the best in others

is a way to reinforce

your own best self.

Greet everyone you meet

with joy in your heart.

One of life's great joys

is the discovery

of who you really are.

When joy springs forth

within your mind,

go deeply into the feeling.

Open your consciousness

and let the light of joy flow in.

Joy is without price.

It comes from accepting life

as it is in the moment.

Joy comes from

an appreciation of life.

BABY'S BREATH

Your joy, love, and laughter

send angels chasing after

every discord to replace it

with a chord of harmony.

Joy grows side by side with love.

The more joy you have,

The more you are able

to give and receive love.

Cultivate joy until your heart

becomes a field of love.

Joy thrives in a climate of harmony.

Joy begets a feeling of relaxation,

a carefreeness that releases burdens

and embraces a sense of freedom

that opens the door

to their resolution.

Joy softens your energy

by promoting a relaxation

of tension and worry.

This frees you to feel more joy,

more life, more love.

Joy

is the laughter of angels.

If your heart is full

of joy and love,

you more easily overlook

shortcomings in others.

Like the sun's nourishing rays,

your joy can nourish

everyone around you.

As you gain wisdom

and transcend your former self,

the nature of your joy

also becomes fuller

and more transcendent.

When you are in tune with

your reason for being,

you become more effective,

spontaneous, and enthusiastic.

You are on fire with joy

and you convey joy to others.

You can recognize intuition,

inspiration, and hunches

by the joy you feel

when they come to you.

Joy is a sign that your higher self

is speaking to you.

Retain your joy

as you move with

the currents of life.

When you have real joy,

every system of your body

and all your internal organs

are filled with joy.

You feel upbeat and confident,

and you radiate an inner glow.

The memory of feeling joy

can reinvigorate you

and give you the ability

to meet the challenges

of the present.

Keep your heart full of joy.

Joy helps to heal illness, depression,

and so many other problems.

The positive spin of joy

supports healing.

Open yourself fully

to the possibility

of a miracle of joy.

Joy has the power to affect

all the cells in your body.

Let your mind become

truly and deeply joyful.

Sometimes a serious illness

sets a person free from struggle.

With nothing to lose,

they determine to spend their days

in activities that bring them joy.

For some, as they regain

a sense of the fullness of life,

health and healing can occur.

This is their miracle of joy.

When you are in a state of joy,

you are in sync with life.

Being in the moment

can boost your joy in living.

Focus on what you have now—

a glorious day, the sun shining,

a true friend, something beautiful.

Live your life

with an expectation

of gladness and joy.

Take a stand for joy!

Look for the joy in every

happening, every occurrence.

Keep your reservoir of joy so full

that where you see nonjoy

you can fill the empty cup.

Look forward with joy

to the surprises life holds.

Trust that the future

will bring you joys and delights.

THE WATERFALL

Happy is the man who entertains

a perpetual spirit of joy,

for his spirit is like

the sun shining at its zenith.

When you experience joy or bliss,

it comes from the cycling

of your consciousness

over and over in patterns of joy

that return ever more joy to you.

Joy accompanies those who live

in harmony with their inner truth.

The energy of joy is intense,

like the dancing of a flame,

and it keeps you balanced.

For the miracle of joy

to work fully for you,

learn to amplify feelings of joy.

When your soul is thrilled

by seeing the first rays

of the sun at dawn,

pink and then gold,

go deeply into that feeling.

Let yourself feel joyful excitement

about the good things you see.

Let feelings of joy spread

in ripples throughout your body.

By doing this again and again,

you accustom your nerve pathways

to the feeling of joy.

Allow joy to well up within

your body, emotions, and mind.

Allow joy to wash away the debris

of doubt, fear, and worry.

When you embrace joy,

the very cells of your body

spin positively.

Make a list of things

that bring you joy.

Affirm them often.

Find ways to return

to that place of joy.

Joy is not a permanent feeling

of happiness all day long.

It is an inner essence,

a steady feeling of peace

and contentment

sustained by the presence

of the Divine within you.

Do you have the steady, healthy joy

that comes from knowing

that a spark of the Divine

lives inside of you

and loves you for who you are?

Reflect on this. Accept it.

Live in a state of joy.

Hold on to your joy.

Never condemn yourself

for a mistake—that's like

poking a hole in a water bottle.

Instead, take action to correct

the mistake and move on.

If dark clouds threaten your joy,

strive hard to retain it.

Focus on simple joys

and the satisfaction that comes

from wisdom gained

and lessons learned.

Negative feelings

are often different angles

of a key issue that

you bump into over and over.

Working through that issue

frees your untapped potential

and releases joy in abundance.

A mother who gives birth

knows that great pain

often precedes great joy.

Likewise, suffering

and hardship give us

a way to measure our joys.

Life's travails

make its joys sweeter.

Don't worry about the cause

of your present situation.

Concern yourself

with whether or not

you are responding to it

with full joy, full love,

and your full capability.

When you bring joy to all you do,

the road becomes easier.

Determine that joy will be

the motivating power

in your life.

Whatever your situation,

the joy of living can be

in your brow and in your heart.

Find the spark of joy within.

Protect and kindle that spark

until joy bursts forth.

To keep your joy steady

takes self-mastery.

Now is the acceptable time for joy.

Don't wait for joy to find you—

make joy happen in your life.

When you live in anticipation

of joyful happenings,

your heart remains open

for joy to enter in.

Reclaim the innocence,

the inner sense you had

as a child,

when you would wake up

with joy in your heart and say,

"I can do anything!"

Claim that state of joy today!

Let your inner child,

with all her joy and wonderment,

take you by the hand and lead you.

SPARKLES
OF
SUNLIGHT

Joy is the sun's radiance

upon sparkling waters,

shimmering with all the colors

of the rainbow.

Such splendid moments

bring flow and regeneration.

To be full of life at any age,

give all your love

and share all your joy.

This is how to hold on

to life, love, and joy.

When we feel deep joy

and inner contentment,

that joy permeates our life,

our family, our home.

Joy cannot grow without love.

Where love is absent,

bitterness easily takes root.

To maintain joy in full flower,

give love perpetually to others.

Hold the expectation of joy

in the chalice of your heart.

Your joyful anticipation generates

a tremendous spiritual response.

As good things happen,

joy grows.

Joy is for sharing.

Joy can be the means

to healing the whole world.

Carry joy with you

everywhere you go.

Become a dispenser of joy.

When the joy within you

seems ready to burst into flame,

that is when you have

the power to ignite hearts

and spread joy to all life.

Imagine joy leaping

heart to heart

throughout the world.

Let it start with you.

Be joy!

Spread joy to others.

The more joy you share,

the more fully

will joy come to you.

Joy flows from

and is perpetually renewed

by the flame within your heart.

From the place of deep joy within,

visualize the entire world

receiving ripples of joy.

When joy fills you like a brook

overflowing its banks,

good things flow more freely.

Be a living fountain of joy.

Meet every adversity

with the rejoicing that

God will see you through it.

When you are in

a difficult situation

don't identify with

the sense of struggle.

Just keep serving the good

and trust in goodness

to see you through to joy.

The uplift you feel

when you share

heart to heart with someone

comes from the joy

of connecting with

their real self.

Hold on to inner joy,

not only in happy times

but in times of burden,

so that you can uplift another

with a cup of joy freely given.

Whatever you are doing,

if you do not feel joy,

look inside.

Get to the bottom of it.

Live your life with joy

and contentment.

To know sweet simplicity in life

is to know profound,

unmitigated joy.

Put joy in every heart,

in every pocket,

and you will be planting seeds

that will multiply

throughout the earth.

Gardens of the Heart Series

Compassion

Gratitude

Forgiveness

Joy

Jardines del corazón

Compasión

Gratitud

Perdón

Alegría

For other titles by
Elizabeth Clare Prophet,
please visit

www.SummitUniversityPress.com